"WOULD YOU RATHER...?" GAME BOOK

by
Mark Cassell

There's only **ONE** rule:

Ask each other
the questions
and explain why.

Have fun!

Published in Great Britain
Copyright © 2021 Megapode Books
Cover and Content Copyright © 2021 Mark Cassell
Images by Vecteezy.com & Pngkey.com
All rights reserved

ISBN: 9798711425120

"Would you rather ...?"

... always have to walk with your hands in the air

or

shout at the top of your lungs rather than talking?

"Would you rather ...?"

... have freezing showers for a year

or

have no phone for two months?

"Would you rather ...?"

… eat a bowl of
brussel sprouts

or

lick the mud from under
a plant pot
for 5 minutes?

"Would you rather ...?"

... wake up every day to an air horn in your face

or

have armpits that always smell of broccoli?

"Would you rather …?"

… be able to talk to animals

or

control the weather?

"Would you rather …?"

… live on the Moon

or

live on Mars?

"Would you rather …?"

… be invisible

or

read minds?

"Would you rather ...?"

... drink only water for a year

or

never eat pizza again?

"Would you rather …?"

… have breakfast with a superhero

or

lunch with a villain?

"Would you rather ...?"

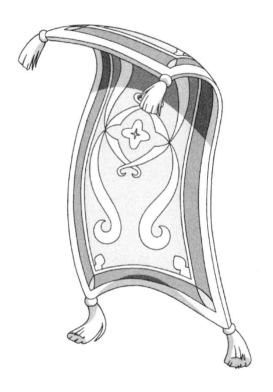

... have a magic carpet?

or

a personal robot?

"Would you rather …?"

… kiss a MASSIVE frog

or

hug an
even bigger snake?

"Would you rather …?"

… have a year of no TV

or

a year without sweets and candy?

"Would you rather …?"

… go 100 years into the past

or

100 years into the future?

"Would you rather …?"

… have a pet dragon

or

a pet dinosaur?

"Would you rather …?"

… meet your favourite singer

or

movie star?

"Would you rather …?"

… be a dog

or

a cat?

"Would you rather ...?"

... have 5 sisters

or

5 brothers?

"Would you rather …?"

… constantly ITCH

or

constantly SNEEZE?

"Would you rather ...?"

... stand in a bucket of eyeballs

or

brains?

"Would you rather …?"

… be locked in an amusement park

or

in a library?

"Would you rather ...?"

… eat a plate of snails

or

sardines?

"Would you rather …?"

… work for a company that makes movies

or

music?

"Would you rather ...?"

... constantly hear the thoughts of animals

or

humans?

"Would you rather ...?"

... sew all your own clothes for the rest of your life

or

have to grow your own food?

"Would you rather ...?"

... only have one eye
in the middle of your forehead

or

have two noses?

"Would you rather …?"

… live in the Sahara Desert

or

in Antarctica?

"Would you rather …?"

… own your own boat

or

plane?

"Would you rather …?"

… give up social media
for the rest of your life

or

have the same dinner
for the rest of your life?

"Would you rather ...?"

... constantly have
wet armpits

or

a runny nose?

"Would you rather …?"

… live on a desert island

or

live in the jungle?

"Would you rather …?"

… have a pause button

or

a rewind button
on your life?

"Would you rather …?"

… breathe fire every time you speak

or

have everything you touch break?

"Would you rather …?"

… never age

or

never sleep?

"Would you rather …?"

… have webbed hands

or

webbed feet?

"Would you rather …?"

… be a character in your favourite book

or

favourite movie?

"Would you rather …?"

… wear a swimming costume for the rest of your life?

or

a clown costume?

"Would you rather …?"

… have a tiny house on a nice street

or

a mansion in a not-too nice neighbourhood?

"Would you rather …?"

… have reptile scales

or

a beak?

"Would you rather …?"

… cartwheel everywhere you go

or

hop like a rabbit?

"Would you rather …?"

… have the ability to breathe under water

or

be able to fly?

"Would you rather ...?"

... be royalty during medieval times

or

middle class in the future?

"Would you rather …?"

… wear gloves all the time

or

a hat?

"Would you rather …?"

… be 12 feet tall

or

12 inches tall?

"Would you rather …?"

… have your favourite singer / movie star vomit on you

or

you vomit on them?

"Would you rather ...?"

... be a mermaid/merman

or

a centaur?

"Would you rather ...?"

... live on a canal boat

or

in an RV for the rest of your life?

"Would you rather ...?"

... have the power to move things with your mind (telekinesis)

or

the ability to read people's minds (telepathy)?

"Would you rather …?"

… communicate with aliens

or

be able to speak all languages on Earth?

"Would you rather ...?"

... live without TV

or

live without your phone?

"Would you rather …?"

… smell like rotten eggs

or

sour milk?

"Would you rather ...?"

... be well known for your intelligence

or

your good looks?

"Would you rather ...?"

... always have bad B.O.

or

be able to smell everyone else's B.O.?

"Would you rather …?"

… own a time machine

or

a teleporter?

"Would you rather …?"

… swim in a pool of slime

or

peanut butter?

"Would you rather ...?"

... have a third arm

or

ridiculously long arms?

"Would you rather ...?"

... your only means of transportation is a giant pig

or

miniature giraffe?

"Would you rather …?"

… chew on a dirty dish cloth

or

eat the dirt from
under the cooker?

"Would you rather ...?"

… be born without knees

or

elbows?

"Would you rather …?"

… be reincarnated as an elephant

or

a giraffe?

"Would you rather …?"

… have smelly feet

or

hair that smells
of soggy cabbage?

"Would you rather …?"

… drink fish tank water

or

eat dog food?

"Would you rather ...?"

... be a teacher at your school

or

the janitor?

"Would you rather …?"

… have bright purple horns

or

bright purple teeth?

"Would you rather …?"

… be the best player on
a losing team

or

the worst player on
the winning team?

"Would you rather …?"

… live in the sky

or

under the sea?

"Would you rather …?"

… have a pig nose

or

snake eyes?

"Would you rather ...?"

... sleep on a bed of dead bugs

or

eat a handful of live worms?

"Would you rather …?"

… go into space

or

go to the bottom of the sea?

"Would you rather …?"

… have unpredictable fainting spells

or

run along an alligator's back,
from tail to head?

"Would you rather ...?"

... have a tail

or

an extra finger?

"Would you rather ...?"

… ride on the back of a T-Rex

or

a sabre-toothed tiger?

"Would you rather …?"

… have no hot water
for the rest of your life

or

no heating?

"Would you rather …?"

… lick a toad for 5 minutes

or

sniff both of your friend's armpits after they've run a marathon?

"Would you rather …?"

… be on a soap opera

or

a game show?

"Would you rather …?"

… have milk tears

or

chocolate toenails?

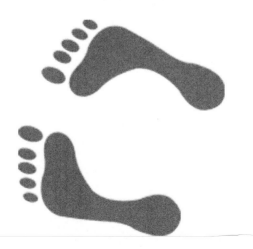

"Would you rather …?"

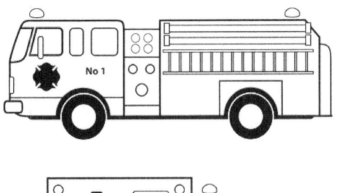

… drive a fire engine

or

an ambulance?

"Would you rather …?"

… own a bakery

or

a coffee shop?

"Would you rather …?"

… live without music

or

movies?

"Would you rather ...?"

... wear winter clothes

or

summer clothes
all year round?

"Would you rather …?"

… be completely bald

or

totally covered in hair?

"Would you rather …?"

… only ever eat
pizza for the rest of your life

or

ice cream?

"Would you rather ...?"

... smell bad

or

always say something embarrassing around the person you have a crush on?

"Would you rather ...?"

… discover a living dinosaur

or

hidden treasure?

"Would you rather …?"

… own a mansion but can only ever use public transport

or

own a private jet but live in a tent?

"Would you rather …?"

… always
smell of onions

or

have a tarantula living in your hair?

"Would you rather ...?"

... be allergic to chocolate

or

chips?

"Would you rather ...?"

... always have a booger that whistles when you breathe

or

always have food stuck between your two front teeth?

"Would you rather …?"

… have stupidly tiny feet

or

ridiculously large hands?

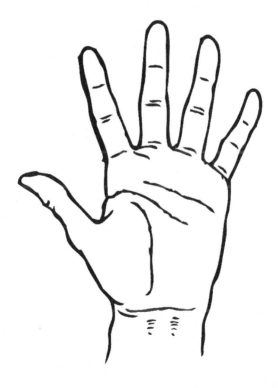

"Would you rather …?"

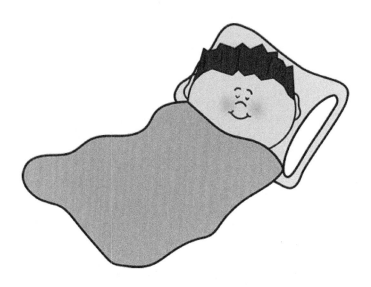

… sleep on a roof during a storm

or

in the basement during a heatwave?

"Would you rather …?"

… always speak in rhyme

or

sing?

"Would you rather ...?"

… do a month of housework

or

eat a pickled onion with every meal
for a whole week?

"Would you rather …?"

… wear fairy wings to school for a week

or

wear a clown's nose?

"Would you rather …?"

… sweat ketchup

or

never have ice cream again?

"Would you rather ...?"

... be slapped across the face with a wet fish

or

be farted on?

"Would you rather …?"

… fight an ostrich

or

a kangeroo?

"Would you rather ...?"

… wear pyjamas
for the rest of your life

or

your grandmother's clothes
to school every day?

"Would you rather ...?"

… have a bath of mushy peas

or

have armpits that
smell bad for a week?

"Would you rather ...?"

... want it to be Summer forever

or

Winter?

"Would you rather ...?"

... count to 10 with your face
in wet bread

or

in cold baked beans?

Printed in Great Britain
by Amazon